California Luxury Living
A Private Tour
John Finton

"Live your Dreams"

CONTENTS

Introduction

If there's one thing I've always wanted, it's to know more. From an early age I could never sit still, could never understand something by merely being told about it—I had to go, see, touch, and experience whatever was out there. I've come to find a challenge suits me fine—I crave excellence. By utilizing and unmasking the talents of the world's top craftspeople and nature's raw elements, I've found building is the language that allows me to participate in the conversation of life. What I'm going to show you—these buildings, these magnificent homes—are the fruits of my labor, the artifacts from my journeys to find the highest-quality materials and orchestrate a reality of what began as a vision on paper: these are my adventures in building.

I've never had an easy time following the crowd or conforming to the standards of life, which has ultimately been a blessing, but was by no means an easy place to start from. By the time I was 21, I had been living on my own for six years, lived in many cities, and started my own construction company a year before graduating from college.

Adopted from an orphanage as infants, my sister and I had everything we could need from wonderful, loving parents. However, they were in their late 30s when they adopted us, and years later, when I entered my teenage years and began to unleash my ambitious curiosity on the world, I was too much for my parents to handle. For example, when I was 13, I heard San Francisco was

amazing, so I got on a bus and went to see it for myself. Misinterpreted and most exhausting, I ended up in the foster care system where the courts would determine my care.

I was in the foster care system for a few months until an old neighbor of my adopted parents, who had always understood and liked me, heard of my predicament and took me in. It was there where I was allowed to be myself, to explore and to ultimately discover and embrace that independence was the only route for me to take. One thing I'd been taught was to always work to have enough money to support myself. So I always held down part time jobs as I traveled— either as a carpenter or a waiter or, finally making it into the mountains, as a ski instructor. I also found I loved to travel, camp, hitchhike, hop on the bus, and meet new people. For years I moved throughout Southern California to Colorado, up to Wyoming, through Nevada to Northern California and finally back home to Los Angeles.

It was during this time I found what inspired me the most was the humbling experience of being in the great outdoors, exposed and at one with the raw elements, and then moving indoors, the way a space can affect us, and we, in turn, can affect that space. I suppose it's no surprise that architecture would later become a fascination of mine—and one in which I'd fervently want to participate.

At 21, when I came back to Southern California, I started taking classes part-time at community college while also taking the bus every day to work part-time at a printing company and occasionally a building project, to pay for it. After transferring, I met a girl in my classes who happened to be the daughter of a renowned Los Angeles interior designer. Kind and generous, they welcomed me into their home and it was there I had a first look at what high-end building could be—and I couldn't get enough of it. Side projects of kitchen renovations and roofing jobs immediately took a back seat while her father allowed me to build a whole room of a home. I had never had a chance to build something from the ground up with such high-quality materials before, and quickly wanted more. By my senior year of college, I had begun buying, renovating, and selling houses locally, was overseeing projects throughout Newport Beach, bought my dream car to get myself from job sites and back to classes as quickly as possible, and somehow had officially begun my own construction company. There was no going back from there, I was hooked—I'd found a way to contribute to the stream of life where I could stay endlessly curious.

After graduating from college, most of my friends either didn't know what they wanted to do or were applying for a decent salaried job; I'd never worked for anyone else and couldn't see myself starting now. I'd come a long way from the 15-year-old who took a second job working on a construction site one summer, so I kept going. I knew California well, and had already begun learning the ropes of various local building standards, city permits, inspections, and specifications for a site's geology. It was only after learning the dance of all these procedures and encountering more and more quality architecture that I began to realize the better the home I built, the higher quality the materials should be. I couldn't possibly sign a contract to erect a building that wasn't durable or didn't look like it was meant to, so I began to wander further throughout the U.S. to seek the best possible materials for the clients I had.

I didn't have a passport until I was 30 years old. In the last 18 years I've traveled to around 70 countries on the search for superior building materials for every client I've had. Seeking out salvaged wood, antique Moroccan tiles or inspecting the infinite types of stone that could be the right fit for a residence, I've taken flights to quarries in desolate fields of France, trains into the mountains of Italy, a six-hour car ride to rural Pennsylvania, dodged bird 'flu in Shenzhen, China, overcome pneumonia on a train ride through Lyons, France, to name just a few. I never know what I'm going to find, but I'm determined and have always found something perfect to bring back.

Aside from a love of the chase, motivation to keep searching for only the best materials comes from the unfaltering humility nature brings. Sure, it's a great ride to paddle surf, to ski, or to hunt in the mountains—but it is also breathtaking to stand over a massive hole in the ground, to watch men cut blocks of stone the size of an Escalade directly from the earth and to decide whether that stone can be the perfect element to actualize the vision of a residence's architecture. Often, if the character and species is right, I have to go to see for myself if a quarry is even large enough to supply all the stone I'd need. What's more is the utter satisfaction of traveling to these distant and unexpected locations to inspect rare or hidden materials and bring them back and work them flawlessly into the building. Doing a final walkthrough with a homeowner before they move in and seeing their reaction to how we've brought a design to life is priceless. Every time I'm reenergized; excited to break ground again and take on the next project. There is nothing like this process.

These homes you see are prized treasures to each of their owners—dwellings that provide them a touchstone for peace and comfort. I am proud to have built these destinations for people to enjoy and cherish, buildings that are monolithic and will stand the test of time for generations to come. Home should always be a sanctuary, a place of comfort. But it's funny—there are as many different visions and ideas about comfort as there are people in the world. What would home or your favorite getaway be without color and light? Without your favorite natural elements or piece of art? Or without those who fill it?

Perhaps it's because I've been traveling alone for so long that I've come to appreciate sharing my adventures with those I love the most. Today, without my family to share my journeys with, it's not the same. My wife and children are my home. Success to me is about letting life in and living it with those I love. As fate would have it, my love of the hunt for that something special has afforded me a priceless reality: I get to travel with my own family, to experience the world with them.

And with my family as my own foundation, I've been given the opportunity to exercise my passions and play conductor to the orchestra of building. Each of the stunningly talented architects and designers I've had the privilege to work with write the music, share their vision, and entrust me to seek out the instruments and artists that will bring the song to life. In these pages are my symphonies—I hope you enjoy them.

Cutting Edge
Contemporary
Beverly Hills, CA
22,000 Sq. Ft.

ARCHITECT: LANDRY DESIGN GROUP, INC., INTERIOR DESIGNER: MAGNI DESIGN

Energetic, light and open, this masterfully detailed 22,000-square-foot contemporary home made the perfect summer retreat for an esteemed homeowner. The precise lines and cutting-edge angles, created with the abundance of Beverly Hills' natural light and curtain walls of glass, greet the senses for a relaxing and luxurious stay in this residence.

With the homeowner's penchant for excellence, and the exciting ventures that come with a flawless modern design, I had a unique mission ahead of me to seek out the homeowner's most important requirement for this property: a hand-chiseled stone from India he simply could not go without. In India, I was pointed to a master carver who sat with a chisel and mallet and etched out hundreds of thousands of rows of lines into the side of each piece of the stone. The lines were so fine that up close it looked like someone had taken a fine-tooth comb and pulled it through the side of the rock. This technique gives a richness and depth to the color, texture and presence of the stone that is like nothing I've seen before. Unless you stand directly in front of the stone, you almost wouldn't know someone sat down to hand-carve each piece. The process is incredibly

THE EXCEPTIONAL INDIAN STONE GREETS YOU FROM THE

EXTERIOR AND WELCOMES YOU THROUGH THE ENTRY

expensive and time-consuming generally, but with such a volume of the material to be used for so much of the residence, inside and out, I was off to find the best possible way to make it work.

After some research I found there was a workshop in China that was manufacturing the product. The raw material was shipped from India to China for expert hand-chiseling, done in mass quantities by hundreds of workers. Upon completion, the bulk of custom-carved stone was then shipped from China to Los Angeles to be installed.

As the exceptional Indian stone greets you from exterior façade and welcomes you in through the entry foyer, it is complemented by the master stair clad entirely in Caesar Stone™. This staircase was incredibly complex to build, curving in unique directions on each floor, with glass sides and steel railings bent very slightly alongside and having to navigate its overall compound radius. The final product was a perfect open passage from one space to the next. The ease and comfort of the home is also enhanced by a home theater and lounge, a vast lawn with an outside lounge and fire pit, a pool with a slide, and a large dining room to host many guests.

THE PRECISE LINES AND CUTTING EDGE

ANGLES GREET THE SENSES FOR A RELAXING STAY

Sweet Escape:
Mizner-Inspired Residence
Beverly Hills, CA
40,000 Sq. Ft.

ARCHITECT: LANDRY DESIGN GROUP INC.   INTERIOR DESIGN: RON WILSON INTERIORS, INC.

Nestled in a lush corner of this Beverly Hills neighborhood, this home resembles an exotic, serene retreat from the world where family can gather and relax, as the owner envisioned. As family was the focal point, the design of the estate was to allow a sense of ease moving from one space to the next, and to have many of those spaces be for abundant entertaining.

Applying materials to the Mizner-esque and Mediterranean Revival feel of the estate, we sourced more natural materials than for any home I've built to cover the 40,000-square-foot property in limestone. No less than 150 containers of limestone—quarried in the Dijon region of France, and milled in six Parisian factories—were used to construct the awe-inspiring façade. Limestone is also used thoughtfully throughout the home in multiple architectural details such as the fireplaces and patios.

Keeping with the home's tropical, resort-like energy, the estate is scattered with palm trees, an entryway fountain, vast lawns and a man-made lake. Curving past a serene fountain, through the motor court, the estate's elegant entryway was architecturally designed to be intimate and warm as you are led through the front door, into a striking two-story, 2,000-square-foot entry foyer whose entire ceiling is a retractable sunroof, making the room feel more like an open air atrium. To balance many of the abundant open spaces and still offer a sense of privacy and comfort, the architect also cleverly created intimate spaces for the homeowner to utilize, such as the two-story mahogany library, the outdoor covered loggia, and multiple areas for lounging and taking in the property's breathtaking views. Between my visits in France to Dijon and Paris overseeing the resourcing of limestone for the property, I also traveled to Morocco, where we gathered inspiration for the design of the doors and lighting fixtures for the home.

To accommodate the homeowner's desire for the utmost ease and comfort of having everything he could want for his family in one place, we implemented multiple entertainment facilities including a 35-millimeter equipped home theater, a bowling alley, a massage room, and a 5,000-square-foot roof deck with a sweeping view of the Los Angeles basin. The interiors in each room of the home are elegant, warm, and sophisticated. Combined, the natural materials, reclaimed details, architecture, and amenities succeed in creating paradise.

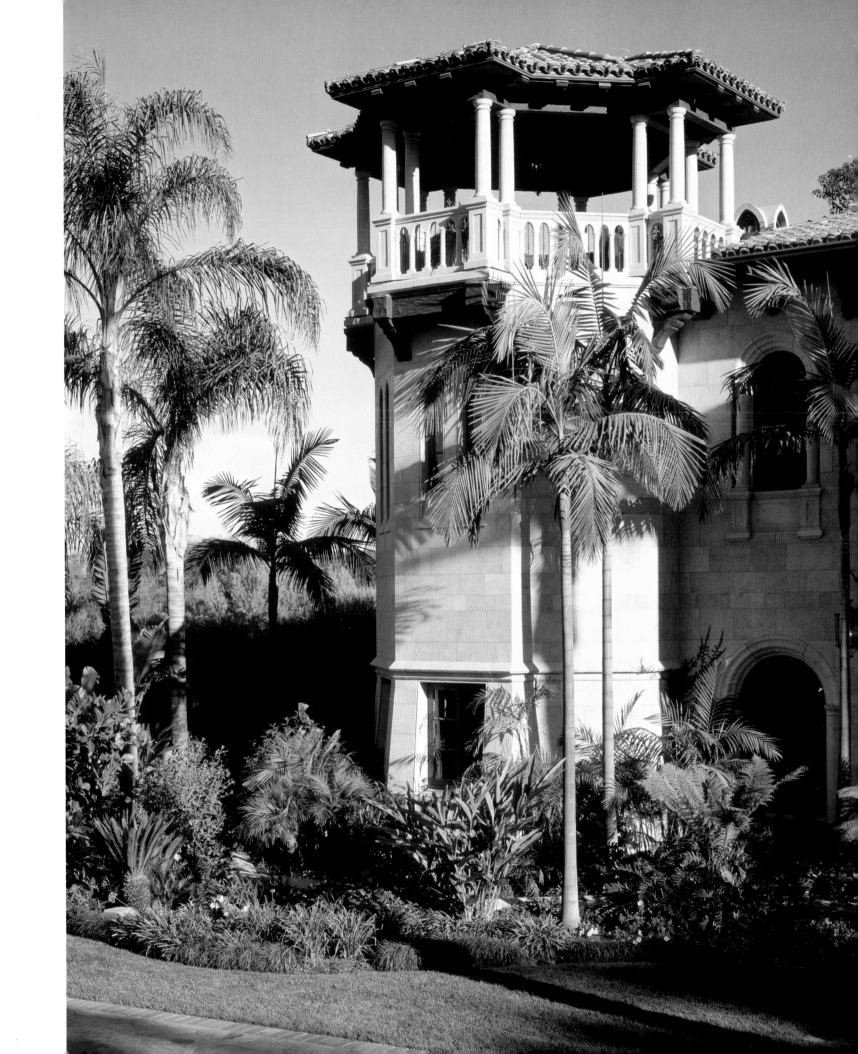

THE INTERIORS IN EACH ROOM OF THE HOME
ARE ELEGANT, WARM AND SOPHISTICATED

Modern Minimalism:
Contemporary Renovation
Beverly Hills, CA
7,000 Sq. Ft.

INTERIOR DESIGNER: MAGNI DESIGN

Nestled in the exclusive Trousdale Estates—celebrity enclave and architectural haven since the 1950s—this Beverly Hills neighborhood was an incredible place to renovate a modern 1960s house into a contemporary, minimalist sanctuary. The homeowner, a 26-year-old entrepreneur and first-time buyer, wanted an open, crisp space to unwind and showcase his art and car collection.

Sitting atop Los Angeles, with panoramic city, canyon, and ocean views, the designer refocused the blueprint of this 7,000-square-foot, single-story house to remain elegant and understated while emphasizing the breathtaking view and surrounding natural elements.

Yet again working with a contemporary design, we had to be meticulous and prepared for all the details. The designer of this renovation was already ahead of the game, examining all proportions to determine what would be in keeping with the structure's integrity and ambiance, even holding regular meetings to be sure alignment was correct down to the furnishings. It was a successful design as the simple, clean, white details and minimal hardware or clutter create a museum-quality

canvas across the residence. To amplify the quality of the backdrop, the solid gallery walls are made from white Thassos Stone from Greece and Eurostone from Italy. The kitchen is also simple and elegant, made up of stainless steel and oak detailing.

Visitors are greeted by a cantilevered walkway that floats above a reflecting pool, leading them through an immaculate, open stone colonnade to the glass front door, looking straight out over the view. Everything about the residence is transparent and beautiful. The front door opens onto the dining and living space that is merely separated from the patio and infinity pool by a wall of sparse columns and large glass panels. Glass also wraps around the master bedroom and master bath, looking out over the patio and sprawling views, allowing you to forget you are inside.

This project was the continuation of another builder's work; the process of disassembling the existing work and starting over took 14 months. The final product was a tranquil and geometrically brilliant building that the homeowner happily occupies.

SIMPLE, CLEAN DETAILS CREATE A MUSEUM

QUALITY CANVAS OF THE RESIDENCE

GLASS WRAPS AROUND THE MASTER BEDROOM AND

BATH, ALLOWING YOU TO FORGET YOU WERE INSIDE

Beaux Arts Inspired
Classical Residence
Beverly Hills, CA
35,000 Sq. Ft.

ARCHITECT: BIGLIN ARCHITECTURAL GROUP, INC.

In the heart of Beverly Hills, the estate that once sat on the prime two-acre Sunset Boulevard lot, home to a long list of prominent occupants, mysteriously burned down in 1980, leaving the site empty. What you see there today is a one-of-a-kind Beaux-Arts inspired palace we completed in just three years, by putting a crew of 100 men to work every day.

The homeowner wanted this prized property to bring a slice of old world Parisian opulence to life, so we made sure every last inch of this three-floor, 32,000-square-foot home was fit for a king. The designer drew much inspiration for the detailing from the George V Hotel in Paris, so it was to Paris we went to source the bulk of our materials.

As this residence was to be no less than the Harry Winston of interiors, each of the home's carefully constructed six bedrooms and bathrooms and a full basement are lavishly adorned with one million dollars' worth of 24-karat gold gilded lights, moldings, and fixtures. Antique chandeliers throughout the home add to the lavish and dynamic detailing, especially in the entry foyer and 800-square-foot master bedroom and bathroom. In the master bathroom, built-in heated mirrors are featured as well as three spacious walk-in closets. Rémy Garnier, responsible for renovating

Versailles' hardware, also elegantly decorates this home, clad in 24-karat gold. Classical detailing also resonates throughout the home's delicate French gardens—complete with custom-carved stone fountains and bird baths—a pool pavilion, tennis court, and even the elevator to the underground 15-car garage.

Fortifying the exterior to exude both elegance and strength, we used a Portuguese limestone. Each separate ornate stone detail was hand-carved by a locally renowned stonemason, and then sent to China for specialty mass duplication. I forged through what was then the bird 'flu epidemic on my first ever trip to China and made my way to Shenzhen, to personally evaluate the shop that was to perfect each piece of stone for the property. The journey through France to China and back was a wild success and made this home one of fewer than 10 homes in Los Angeles with an entirely hand-cut stone exterior.

This home also includes a music room where the owner—a gospel singer—can showcase his talents. Today, the homeowners thoroughly enjoy throwing open the bronze-clad doors of their home to throw fundraisers and parties.

THE HOMEOWNER WANTED TO BRING A SLICE
OF OLD WORLD PARISIAN OPULENCE TO LIFE

GOLD GILDED LIGHTS, MOLDINGS AND FIXTURES

Incessant Perfection: Modern Residence Beverly Hills, CA 15,000 Sq. Ft.

ARCHITECT: LANDRY DESIGN GROUP, INC., INTERIOR DESIGNER: MAGNI DESIGN

In a cherished Beverly Hills gated community of 50 residences, this property is one of only three contemporary homes. The homeowner wanted a private space that was also fresh and open inside. And so we proceeded to bring to life this clean, cool, and innovative six-bedroom, six-bathroom modern residence that was a harmonious blend of shapes and lines.

This home would be a huge lesson for me, and one that enriched my career exponentially: it was the first contemporary home I would build of this size and scale. With architecture like this, it is plainly unforgiving in honesty and bold openness—but in order to bring contemporary design to life, you must be three steps ahead and not miss a single detail. There is no ornament or detailing to cover mistakes or structural oddities that can arise in a building process—everything shows. I believe this is part of the draw of modern work, the sincerity of each detail. The integrity of open space was paramount to the homeowner, and thus we set out to perfect a list of the few pivotal materials we would use to articulate the originality of the design, and tapped into a limited pool of extremely talented artisans to help us along the way.

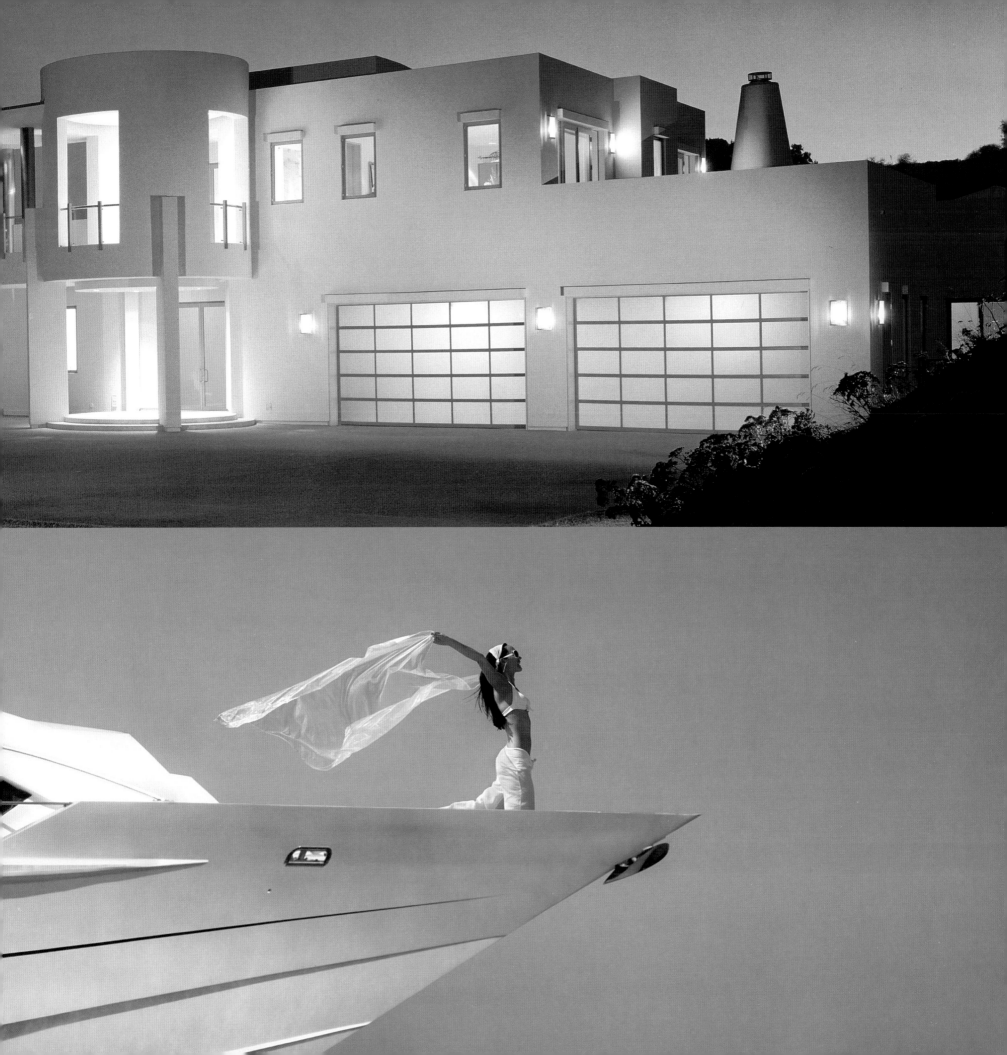

The majority of the residence, including the roof, is composed of Rheinzink, large panels of glass, and stainless steel detailing. The long, rectangular halls and walkways are complemented by circular, intimate spaces such as the breakfast area and master bedroom, which look on to the rest of the property through floor-to-ceiling glass walls. The challenge of both finding suppliers who make glass panels of this size and connecting them with the Rheinzink roof took scrupulous focus, as the smallest error would stand out immensely.

Outside, stainless steel columns, imported from overseas, border the unique second-floor walkway that connects the main residence to the photography studio and gym. Special gaskets had to be installed in the circular areas above the walkway, to account for the extreme daytime heat and nighttime cool, but also wound up giving a unique shadow play to the outdoor area.

Accent materials that warm the sleek cool of steel and glass include doorways wrapped in maple, small Italian tiles surrounding the master shower, and an abundance of stucco and limestone which carries over through the exterior to the interior. The final product of this journey was a balance of chic order and bold style that soothes the senses.

THIS IS PART OF THE DRAW TO MODERN
WORK, THE SINCERITY OF EACH DETAIL

Power House:
French Normandy
Beverly Hills, CA
42,000 Sq. Ft.

ARCHITECT: LANDRY DESIGN GROUP, INC., INTERIOR DESIGNER: JOAN BEHNKE & ASSOCIATES, INC.

Thoughtfully detailed and properly scaled to evoke an old world French ambiance, this architectural gem was a welcome addition to this exclusive Beverly Hills neighborhood.

We staffed 150 people a day to turn this 2.5-acre lot into a 42,000-square-foot *tour de force* in just three years. The exterior façade sets the stage for the lavish visuals to come, composed entirely of salvaged antique stone tiles from France. Young redwood trees were flown in to surround the property's periphery with fresh, sweet air. The remainder of the landscaping, moving in towards the house, was kept minimal to give focus to the architecture.

The greatest challenge, which also made building this project a most exhilarating experience, was sourcing and incorporating more reclaimed materials than I have ever seen used before. Every last material was specially handpicked for this home and tailored to assist in actualizing both the homeowner's dream and the architect's design of it. The entry foyer gives an extravagant welcome, with beams of natural light coming through the elliptical iron webbed skylight and leads in all directions to rooms filled with thoughtful, luxuriant interiors. Lighting, ironwork, and additional antique elements were sought out from numerous Parisian flea markets. The ceilings are composed of aged timber from vintage Irish barns, flawless bronze windows found and shipped from Rimini,

Italy, and extra thick Vermont slate tiles on the roof add a particularly mature, country feel. Also keeping with the old world style of the home, we went back to France to obtain nearly half a dozen period fireplaces and reclaimed French oak for the flooring, which gave each room a warm, vintage feel. It is these continuing architectural details throughout the 42,000-square-foot building that give each room of the home a surprising intimacy.

In keeping with the residence's decadent yet modest ambiance, there is a formal dining room and a professional kitchen, but also a sit-in kitchen in between for the family. We added a loggia nearby with folding doors that lead out to the patio and nearby pool. Upstairs, past the luxurious master suites, a state-of-the-art fitness center and sauna lead out to a balcony, which acts as a bridge, connecting the main structure to the guest quarters. The guest quarters are surrounded on three sides by the main building, and with the bridge attaching the second floor, the two buildings appear as one while also creating small, cobblestone walkways below, reminiscent of Parisian side streets.

Below the main floors, the basement houses a home theater, cigar and billiard room, and a climate-controlled wine cellar with capacity for 2,600 bottles, clad with Dalle de Bourgogne croûte bricks, and which leads through a hidden stair directly up to the dining room for easy access at dinner parties.

GUEST QUARTERS SURROUNDED BY THE
MAIN BUILDING CREATE SMALL WALKWAYS,
REMINISCENT OF PARISIAN SIDESTREETS

THE BASEMENT HOUSES A HOME THEATER, CIGAR AND BILLIARD ROOM, AND A CLIMATE-CONTROLLED WINE CELLAR

A Modernist Take
On French Provençal
Malibu, CA
10,000 Sq. Ft.

ARCHITECT: GIANNETTI ARCHITECTS & INTERIORS, INC., INTERIOR DESIGNER: MADELINE STUART & ASSOCIATES

These homeowners stumbled upon a rarity: an empty, six-acre lot of undeveloped land overlooking the Pacific Ocean and just a stone's throw from Malibu's Zuma Beach. Promptly purchased, with a desire to transform the unruly terrain into their equestrian retreat, it took nearly five years to develop the land properly to then build this 10,000-square-foot, four-bedroom home.

Designed to cater to the homeowners' love of riding and raising horses and the lush natural setting, the residence was to emulate the country homes found in the south of France. Found in France, ideal wood beams were salvaged and used throughout the home's ceilings and carry over into the six-horse stable. To source the appropriate complementary materials, original antique French doors still slightly rusted and maintaining their original mail slots were installed. Santa Barbara sandstone carries throughout the exterior and inside for the flooring to retain the rural feel of the estate.

The property utilizes the vast landscape to create space for outdoor recreational activities such as riding trails that lead down the Pacific Coast Highway, as well as light gardens and sprawling pastures for horses and dogs to roam. Inside, below the main floor's airy layout, the activities continue into the basement entertainment area with a small theater, pinball machines, basketball court, and a reclaimed and rebuilt bowling alley from the 1960s.

Whereas the intention was for this residence to become the homeowners' recreational, equestrian retreat, by the time the building was completed, they decided it was the only place they wanted to be, moving in permanently.

THE RESIDENCE WAS TO EMULATE THE COUNTRY
HOMES FOUND IN THE SOUTH OF FRANCE

Greener Pastures:
17th-Century French Revival
Beverly Hills, CA
22,000 Sq. Ft.

ARCHITECT: HABLINSKI + MANION ARCHITECTURE, LLP, INTERIOR DESIGNER: RICHARD HALLBERG INTERIOR DESIGN

Once again channeling the old world, this property called for another especially thoughtful venture back through time and French architectural history to recreate what this homeowner wanted to be his own old world Parisian country chateau in sunny Los Angeles.

On this seven-acre lot of land we built a grand 22,000-square-foot country home assembled primarily out of materials and techniques that were used in 17th-century France, while weaving in amenities to accommodate the comforts of modern living. Traditional French doors with contemporary screens added to them for functionality open out to the outdoor logia covered in bold, rusticated stone. Inside, the floors of salvaged oak are complemented by antique limestone detailing and similar wood ceiling beams reclaimed from France. The larger the estate, the harder it is to find an ample quantity of salvaged materials for the entire residence—but when the challenge is met, the final aesthetic quality is a priceless reward. The quantity of wood found in France was sizeable, but just short of enough for the entire residence. After some research we were able to find extremely similar beams gauged close to the same size in rural Pennsylvania, and between the two we had enough for the home. It turned out beautifully to have the wood

beams throughout, especially in the library and basement and the homeowners personally requested an attic-office overlooking the property.

For the public spaces in the home I commissioned a classically trained French company to finish the walls with Stuc Pierre, a traditional French plaster alternative to natural cut stone, made from 85 percent limestone aggregate but gypsum-based and easily honed in different styles. Funnily enough it's visible all over Paris and throughout the Louvre alongside actual cut limestone; I just never knew I was looking at it. The same effect is captured throughout the long halls, ornate coved ceilings, and grand two-story foyer in this residence.

And of course, in keeping with the rustic charm theme of the old world, the property's natural landscape, and the beauty of California, this home is conducive to outdoor living. The residence is complete with a pool, an elegant guesthouse, exquisitely landscaped gardens, and behind that a hidden grass tennis court. Offering an esteemed and comforting welcome to the home, two remarkable, custom-crafted iron gates open to lead you through the gravel motor court and up to the front door.

COMPLETE WITH A POOL, ELEGANT GUEST HOUSE, EXQUISITELY

Now and Zen:
Contemporary Renovation
Beverly Hills, CA
13,000 Sq. Ft.

ARCHITECT: BIGLIN ARCHITECTURAL GROUP

In another area of Beverly Hills, this once average addition to the neighborhood's streetscape was revived with water, fire, and stone during a full-scale renovation and addition. The transformation from a typical, traditionally designed house into a minimalist utopia required seamlessly bringing the indoors out and the outdoors in, while utilizing only the best materials for the home's core elements.

Conducive to outdoor living this home features five unique fountains, many adventurously curated adjacent to equally as distinctive fire features, embodying the boldness and tranquility of the estate— a continuous theme throughout the property. The exterior of the home was designed as ethereal and sophisticated as the interior and landscape, tailored to read much like an Armani suit. To achieve this we chose a superlative stone from a quarry just outside of Quebec City, Canada.

There is an indoor and outdoor dining room, living room, and loggia. From the outdoor dining

THE EXTERIOR WAS DESIGNED AS ETHEREAL AND

SOPHISTICATED AS THE INTERIOR AND LANDSCAPE

and living room, designed especially for year-round outdoor use with horizontal shades and a retractable skylight, akin to a convertible top, you can look across the Zen-like back yard toward the guest house and spa. The outdoor rooms feature the use of Ipe wood, which complements the all-white interior nicely, giving an almost resort-like feel to the home.

Much of what further accentuates the indoor/outdoor theme of the interior are the abundant shapes and lines created from the core materials and boundless natural light. To achieve the optimal effect we found windows and doors of the highest quality from the oldest and most renowned window company in the United States. We also sourced fine custom cabinetry from a company in Italy, who sent their own artisan across the seas to perfect every last detail of their installation.

But by far the biggest adventure and challenge creating this home was the production of one of its most beautiful details: pure-white, Greek Thassos stone floors. To create the sweeping beauty of the contemporary, minimalist interior and showcase the owner's art collection, we used a nearly completely white backdrop, and Thassos stone was the highest possible quality material to help achieve this. However, to source the quantity of stone to cover the flooring took nearly a year: only ten percent of the quarry's stone was unblemished, pure white and acceptable for this home, and finding it was tough. I flew to Greece regularly during this project to oversee the harvest and inspection of Thassos super-slabs. However, once we finally sourced enough stone and had it installed, the outcome was unparalleled and worth every trip.

WINDOWS AND DOORS OF THE HIGHEST QUALITY

Seaside Surrender: Traditional Beach Home
Malibu, CA
13,000 Sq. Ft.

ARCHITECT: GIANNETTI ARCHITECTS & INTERIORS, INC.,
INTERIOR DESIGNER: DAVID PHOENIX INTERIOR DESIGN

Situated on three lots of the private Carbon Beach in Malibu, this 13,000-square-foot family home was designed for the comfort and enjoyment of a family's beachside living. The property, which belonged to the former mayor of Los Angeles, was situated in a prestigious neighborhood in which we could make little noise and had even less time to build.

I love a challenge, and what could be a better challenge than time? We overcame the location's geology, the Coastal Commission, building without a sea wall (where the ocean laps up underneath the tennis court and patio), and began pouring concrete and installing 150 caissons, digging more than 100 feet deep into the earth, to create a solid foundation for the property. In a record 16 months we finished what would become the most expensive house to sell in Malibu.

With solid ground beneath us we went on to complete this residence which emulates Catalina Island's 'Tuna Club', blending easily with its ocean front setting. White shingles and white board and batten made from locally reclaimed wood give the home a modern beach house aesthetic. Floors of salvaged French limestone create a smooth transition from outdoors to indoors and Santa Barbara sandstone adds elegance to the relaxed atmosphere. The expansive outdoor patio with a full lounge, top-of-the-line barbecue, fire pit, and swimming pool add just the right scenery for a lifetime of fabulous Southern California family gatherings.

THE EXPANSIVE OUTDOOR PATIO ADDS JUST THE

RIGHT SCENERY FOR A LIFETIME OF FAMILY GATHERINGS

Re-envisioning Renovation:
Historic Modern Estate
Bel Air, CA
8,000 Sq.Ft.

ARCHITECT: FREDERICK FISHER AND PARTNERS ARCHITECTS
INTERIOR DESIGNER: MOORE RUBLE YUDELL ARCHITECTS & PLANNERS

Originally built in 1965 by the renowned modernist architect Archibald Quincy Jones, this 8,000-square-foot Bel Air estate underwent an insightful revision with two small new buildings added to the property. The homeowner, who had excitedly bought the property later on to prevent it from being torn down, decided to add a bit of drama to the history of the estate, snatching up multiple neighboring lots of land to amass a squalling 10 acres of land to create his own vineyard.

When going in to build on a historic property such as this we had to be extremely mindful of our movements. The homeowner had an incredible collection of art which was showcased throughout the house and tearing out walls and rooms to create new spaces takes

a masterful hand not to damage the existing anatomy of the building—much like restoring a classic car to its original grandeur but with modern comforts.

Visitors enter through a sycamore-lined, Italian gravel drive and continue through 11-foot-high, bright red doors made from the same translucent acrylic as the interior's bright, primary colored panels. A beautiful trio of Robert Graham bronze figures in the sculpture court play elegantly with the concrete and steel of the home's exterior. The home's floor plan is wide open with beaming natural light coming through the floor-to-ceiling glass walls, rift-sawn white oak flooring, and granite master bath. A re-plastered fireplace separates the entry from both sides of the living area and a bulthaup kitchen from Germany makes for a perfect accompaniment to the homeowners' full-time chef.

TEARING OUT WALLS TAKES A MASTERFUL HAND

NOT TO DAMAGE THE EXISTING BUILDING

Best Kept Secret:
Modern Retreat
Carpinteria, CA
6,000 Sq. Ft.

ARCHITECTURE & INTERIOR DESIGN: MOORE RUBLE YUDELL ARCHITECTS & PLANNERS

Drawn to Southern California's beautiful beaches, this homeowner leapt at the chance to buy a quirky 1970s dwelling located on this priceless oceanfront enclave. What began as a desire to make a few topical changes to the existing 6,000-square-foot estate morphed into a full-scale renovation. An ocean-front home comes with ample tranquility within, but the elements can be harsh on the materials—this transformation was to be one of immense precision and unprecedented durability. Bringing in a crew of 50 a day, we tore down the existing structure and built this timeless contemporary gem from the ground up in a record seven months.

Clad in rustic Cedar shingles, the front of the building appears to be one of an understated East Coast aesthetic. With an almost cozy driveway carved out of the modest wooden façade you would not suspect that inside and spilling out to the patio and beachfront was a sleek, sophisticated modern haven.

When walking through the pivoting, bright red front door (the only bold colored detail in the home) into a two-story entry, you're greeted by a dramatic, steel-railed catwalk that leads off to the bedrooms or, in the other direction, the office and outdoor patio. With zero time and no room for error, we also added a kitchen terrace, outdoor fireplace, and large master bathroom with a curtain glass wall overlooking the spectacular ocean view. In keeping with the otherwise neutral color palette of the home, we chose a bleached, white plank oak for the flooring throughout. Just as promptly as we finished, this became the homeowner's favorite weekend getaway.

WITH A MODEST FAÇADE YOU WOULD NOT SUSPECT

WE ADDED A MASTER BATHROOM WITH A CURTAIN GLASS

WALL OVERLOOKING THE SPECTACULAR OCEAN VIEW

Classical Italian meets
French Art Deco
Beverly Hills, CA
22,000 Sq. Ft.

ARCHITECT: LANDRY DESIGN GROUP, INC., INTERIOR DESIGNER: JOAN BEHNKE & ASSOCIATES, INC.

On a rare piece of real estate in Beverly Hills, these homeowners were dedicated to having a sophisticated, one-of-a-kind home to fill with family and warmth—and this is exactly what they got. The Italian architecture and façade of the building is juxtaposed beautifully with a unique French Art Deco interior. Staffing 100 workers a day, we built this seven-bedroom, 22,000-square-foot residence from the ground up in just three years.

As the design called for a natural-cut stone exterior, I was back in France searching out the best material. Somewhere between Paris, Dijon, and an overnight train to Lyons I caught pneumonia but made it through a tour of quarries just in time to both get well again and realize that French limestone from the Dijon region was the best fit. Once again we used the talents of the workshop in Shenzhen, China to hand-carve the large quantity of stone and had it sent back to Los Angeles to create the new building.

We hired a skilled plaster atelier from New York to create the custom-scalloped walls of the entry foyer and the architectural detailing of the second-floor, open-air atrium. The endless windows throughout the residence were brought in from Rimini, Italy. Across from the atrium

is the entrance to the master suite, which opens onto an elegant sitting room, bedroom, and his-and-her master bathrooms, each clad with sultry, smart antique décor. The homeowners fell in love with an Italian marble that we wanted to use on more of the house, but only a limited quantity was left in existence. Chasing the remaining blocks of stone took a few trips to the Tuscan coast. Finally, when on a cruise with my family not far from the area the stone came from, I had to leave the boat a couple days for one last look. During the brief excursion I found and purchased the remaining blocks of marble and they fit perfectly as a core element in the hearth of the master sitting room.

As one of the most important uses for this home was to gather the homeowners' large family, we worked closely alongside the designer and architect to create the finest entertainment areas. A large dining room for formal meals overlooks the front landscape, while a spacious and meticulously planned kitchen sits adjacent to an informal breakfast room. To be sure the homeowners had the best experience of their love of culinary arts, I traveled to Italy with the interior designer for the perfect kosher granite counters for the kitchen. The family room nearby offers serene comfort with a lounge and built-in aquarium.

The activities continue downstairs with a spa containing an indoor pool, hot tub, massage suite, and sauna. For more enlivening gatherings you're led to the one-of-a-kind game room, designed to emulate the deck of a 1930s ocean-liner, complete with rope chandeliers, a steel-framed ceiling, and a unique *trompe l'oeil* custom-painted mural across the main wall, giving the genuine ambiance of a ship's deck. Also downstairs, a home theater and wine cellar with room for 1,500 bottles also make for wonderful entertainment.

Outside, we built the swimming pool and added a two-story guesthouse with a small outdoor lounge with a fire pit that overlooks the pool and the elegant rear façade of the main house.

Acknowledgements

Having never been involved in the creation of a book before, I had no idea how much work was involved. I would like to thank Jill Cohen, my book agent, for the time she spent helping make my dream a reality. I would also like to thank my branding expert Penelope Francis for helping me make the right choices; your guidance is greatly appreciated.

I would also like to thank Doug Turshen and Steve Turner for their brilliant design and Alanna Bailey and Samantha Kopf for their invaluable help with the text.

Additionally, I would like to thank my assistant Nicole Gomez for her ability to keep me focused. I would also like to acknowledge my team of Project Managers for the years of hard work and dedication in constructing the homes in the pages of this book. My gratitude extends to the workers, subcontractors, and laborers for their talent and diligence.

It is not easy, but it is a worthwhile task, to build the dream homes for our clients and to materialize the vision of the architects and designers.

Overall, without my wonderful staff and my business partner, Daniel Tontini, I would never have been able to accomplish building over 350 amazing projects in the past 25 years.

Credits

AUTHOR:
Finton Construction
401 Rolyn Place
Arcadia, CA 91007
P: 626.445.1044
www.Finton.com

For appearances or public relations,
please contact:

Penelope Francis
Penelope Francis & Co.
133 South Bedford Drive
Townhouse C
Beverly Hills, CA 90212
P: 310.405.0031
Penelope@penelopefrancis.com
www.PenelopeFrancis.com

DESIGNER CREDITS:

Biglin Architectural Group, Inc.
5115 Douglas Fir Road, Suite M
Calabasas, CA 91302
P: 818.225.2202
www.biglingroup.com

David Phoenix Interior Design
8900 Melrose Avenue, Suite 201
Los Angeles, CA 90069
P: 310.657.6577
www.davidphoenix.com

Frederick Fisher and Partners Architects
12248 Santa Monica Boulevard
Los Angeles, CA 90025
P: 310.820.6680
www.fisherpartners.net

Giannetti Architects & Interiors, Inc.
11980 San Vicente Boulevard
Los Angeles, CA 90049
P: 310.820.1329
www.giannettiarchitects.com

Hablinski + Manion Architecture, LLP
Richard Manion Architecture, Inc.
11150 W. Olympic Boulevard, Suite 800
Los Angeles, California 90064
P: 310.858.8525
www.richardmanion.com

William Hablinski Architecture
75 Beverly Park
Beverly Hills, CA 90210
P: 310.283.5865
www.williamhablinski.com

Joan Behnke & Associates, Inc.
9215 West Olympic Boulevard
Los Angeles, CA 90025
P: 310.446.7738
joan@joanbehnke.com
www.joanbehnke.com

Landry Design Group, Inc.
11333 Iowa Avenue
Los Angeles, CA 90025
P: 310.444.1404
www.landrydesigngroup.com

Madeline Stuart & Associates
717 North La Cienega Boulevard
Los Angeles, CA 90069
P: 310.657.8200
www.madelinestuart.com

Magni Design
8581 Santa Monica Boulevard, Suite 12
Los Angeles, CA 90069
P: 310.623.1623
www.magnidesign.com

Moore Ruble Yudell Architects & Planners
933 Pico Boulevard
Santa Monica, CA 90405
P: 310.450.1400
www.moorerubleyudell.com

Richard Hallberg Interior Design
Designers: Richard Hallberg & Barbara
Wiseley
8720 Melrose Avenue
Los Angeles, CA 90069
P: 310.659.7238
www.hallberg-wiseleydesigners.com

Ron Wilson Interiors, Inc.
8322 Beverly Boulevard, Suite 307
Los Angeles, CA 90048
P: 310.276.0666
www.ronwilsondesigner.com

Published in Australia in 2013 by
The Images Publishing Group Pty Ltd
ABN 89 059 734 431
6 Bastow Place, Mulgrave, Victoria 3170, Australia
Tel: +61 3 9561 5544 Fax: +61 3 9561 4860
books@imagespublishing.com
www.imagespublishing.com

Copyright © The Images Publishing Group Pty Ltd 2013
The Images Publishing Group Reference Number: 1021

National Library of Australia Cataloguing-in-Publication entry:

Author: Finton, John.
Title: California luxury living : a private tour.
ISBN: 9781864704396 (hbk).
Subjects: Architecture—California.
               Architecture—domestic—California.
               Architecture—American influences.
               Architecture—modern—21st century.
Dewey Number: 720.9794

Edited by Driss Fatih

Designed by Doug Turshen with Steve Turner

Pre-publishing services by United Graphic Pte Ltd, Singapore

Printed by Everbest Printing Co. Ltd., in Hong Kong/China on
140gsm GoldEast Matt Art paper

IMAGES has included on its website a page for special notices in relation to this and
our other publications. Please visit www.imagespublishing.com.

Every effort has been made to trace the original source of copyright material contained
in this book. The publishers would be pleased to hear from copyright holders to rectify
any errors or omissions.

The information and illustrations in this publication have been prepared and supplied
by the contributor. While all reasonable efforts have been made to ensure accuracy,
the publishers do not, under any circumstances, accept responsibility for errors,
omissions and representations, express or implied.